A WAY OF THE CROSS

Tolbert McCarroll

A Way of the Cross

with photographs by
Michael Marie Zobelein, O.P.

PAULIST PRESS
NEW YORK/MAHWAH

Acknowledgements

All scriptural texts, except the Psalms,
are taken from *The Jerusalem Bible*. Copyright © 1966
by Darton, Longman & Todd, Ltd. and Doubleday
& Company, Inc.
Used by gracious permission of the publisher.
The prayer accompanying the IV Station is
from *The Book of Common Prayer*, published by the
Church Hymnal Corporation of the Episcopal Church and
officially certified for use in 1979.

The following are quoted by
financial arrangement with the respective publishers.
The Psalms are from the Grail edition (*The Psalms: A New
Translation*, 1963, William Collins Sons & Co.
Ltd., London). The prayer accompanying the
XIII Station is from *A Book of Blessings*,
copyright © 1981, Canadian Conference
of Catholic Bishops, Ottawa, Ontario.

Copyright © 1985 by
Tolbert McCarroll

All rights reserved. No part of this book may be reproduced
or transmitted in any form or by any means,
electronic or mechanical,
including photocopying, recording, or by
any information storage and
retrieval system without permission in writing
from the Publisher.

Library of Congress Catalog Card Number: 84–61025

ISBN: 0–8091–2653–2

Published by Paulist Press
997 Macarthur Boulevard
Mahwah, New Jersey 07430

Printed and bound in the United States of America

Since all people are in fact called to one and the same destiny, which is divine, we must hold that the Holy Spirit offers to all the possibility of being made partners, in a way known to God, in the Paschal Mystery.

> From the Pastoral Constitution on the Church in the Modern World (Vatican II, *Gaudium et Spes*, n. 22).

FOREWORD

The events surrounding the death of Jesus have always been a central concern to his followers. How we reflect upon these moments helps determine our response, not only to our heritage of faith, but also to our present world.

Experience of the Cross

It is not enough to intellectually pursue the evidence surrounding the agony and glory of Jesus. We must do more than construct theological concepts. We feel called to actual participation in the experience. This desire for a personal experience has been present throughout the story of the Christian people. It came to a certain flowering in the Middle Ages with the realization that God had the same desire.

Bernard of Clairvaux in 1119 developed for his monks the now familiar approach that knowledge of ourselves gives rise to an awareness of the needs of others, which in turn leads to compassion, and, eventually, a knowledge of God. He felt so strongly about this process that in a treatise on *The Degrees of Humility and Pride* he had no hesitancy in stating that Jesus relied on the same procedure.

> Such was the example shown by our Savior, who desired to suffer himself in order that he

might learn to feel compassion, and to be afflicted in order that he might learn how to show mercy. . . . Not that the Lord whose mercy is from age to age was ignorant of mercy's *meaning* until then; he knew its nature from all eternity, *but he learned it by personal experience during his days on earth.*

Thus, two different ways of knowing are labeled "meaning" and "personal experience." In the twentieth century we have reshuffled these concepts in psychology, education, philosophy and theology in a variety of ways with many different terms. It is, however, generally accepted that the kind of thinking we use to fill out income tax returns has limitations when applied to trying to understand the overall nature of human existence. Scriptural studies and other scientific explorations increase our *objective knowledge* about Jesus. But when we do this Jesus becomes an "it," that is, something outside of ourselves. Our calculations are linear (step A leads to B, which leads to C) and rational, or at least we hope they are. This corresponds to the specialized function of the left hemisphere of the brain.

On the other end of the scale, or more correctly in the other hemisphere of the brain, we can sometimes obtain a crashing insight into the nature of existence. This *enlightenment*, as Asian spirituality sometimes terms it, is a gift—like wisdom which follows not from calculating mental activity but rather from learning to wait and to listen. What we are trying to know suddenly grasps us and transforms us into itself. Poets and religious sages are most comfortable in this pattern. All of us have some experience with receiving intuitive knowledge. Usually we started out hunting for something and at some point we became the hunted. That which we were attempting to grasp reached out and consumed us. In the most intimate way we participate in the life of that which we sought.

However, for most of us, at least in the Western religions, the most fruitful times of spiritual growth occur in a middle ground which has been termed "existential." Here we do not so much follow behind Jesus as walk side by side with him. He is not an "object" of our investigation but he is a subject like ourselves and we are participating in some way in his existence. Therefore we gain a personal knowledge or *consciousness* of his experience. In Martin Buber's term, we enter into an I-Thou relation. Jesus is no longer outside us as in "objective knowledge," nor is the difference between us totally dissolved, as in "enlightenment." There is a mutuality, a reciprocity, a solidarity between my experience and his. Understanding the essential relationship between grace and consciousness is one of the theological frontiers of our age.

Recognizing that Jesus' death and resurrection is a repetitive theme in our religious history, it becomes our obligation to make his experience live again in our age through our own experience. In this sense history becomes not a series of chapters mechanically beginning at each individual birth and ending at his or her death, but a continuing stream which transcends time.

History of the Devotion

It was in pursuit of this consciousness of the Passion that the pious practice of the Stations of the Cross arose in the early Church. It was an age noted for pilgrimages. By visiting the place where an event occurred the pilgrim hoped to participate more completely in the experience associated with that place or "station" (from the Latin *statio*). Originally the desire was to go to Jerusalem and visit the presumed sites of Jesus' last journey. But this desire was too central to faith to be restricted to adventurers who could afford to visit the Holy Land. Stations were erected in Bologna in the fifth century. In 1342 the Franciscans took over the care of the holy places in Jerusalem. They also began to erect Stations in their European monasteries. The practice quickly spread to parish churches. By the eighteenth century the Way of the Cross had become one of the most popular of devotions in the Roman Catholic Church. Very detailed instructions were given in canon law on how Stations were to be erected. It was obviously considered an important matter.

Which Stations?

Since the sixteenth century there have traditionally been fourteen Stations:

- I Jesus is condemned to death
- II Jesus takes up his cross
- III Jesus falls the first time
- IV Jesus meets his blessed mother
- V The cross is laid on Simon of Cyrene
- VI Veronica wipes the face of Jesus
- VII Jesus falls a second time
- VIII Jesus speaks to the women of Jerusalem
- IX Jesus falls a third time
- X Jesus is stripped of his garments
- XI Jesus is nailed to the cross
- XII Jesus dies on the cross

XIII The body of Jesus is taken down from the cross
XIV The body of Jesus is laid in the tomb

However, in some places there have been as many as thirty-six Stations. In Vienna in the eighteenth century the Stations were reduced to eleven. In Bologna there were five. Traditional Stations III, IV, VI, VII, IX, and XIII were based only on inferences in the Gospels or pious legends. In some Anglican communities these six Stations have been removed, making eight Stations. In former times a fifteenth Station was sometimes added to commemorate Helena's supposed finding of the "true cross." In recent times the resurrection has often been added as a fifteenth Station so as not to disassociate Christ's death from his resurrection.

In the excessively sentimental devotions encouraged in the early part of this century the Way of the Cross occupied a special place. Baroque pictorial representations were sometimes so romantic as to appear to have Jesus physically unaffected by the events taking place around him. The average person had considerable difficulty in relating his or her own life experience to whatever was being so elaborately portrayed. In addition, the dramatic and moralistic productions of some clergymen began to make this a devotion to be avoided, except perhaps in Holy Week or as a penance by which we bargained with a stern God for forgiveness or a special favor.

The gross excesses of people being nailed on crosses or scourging themselves through the streets helped to put all practices associated with the Passion into the category of superstition.

Yet it is a sign of the basic desire of Christians to be in solidarity with this aspect of Jesus' life that the practice of a Way of the Cross is undergoing a revitalization. In some places a new list of Stations have been approved and erected. The Cathedral of SS. Peter and Paul in Clifton (Bristol), England, has the following Stations:

    I Jesus shares the Last Supper with his disciples
   II Jesus prays in the garden
  III Jesus is betrayed and arrested
  IV Jesus is disowned by Peter
   V Jesus is scourged and mocked
  VI Jesus is condemned to death
 VII Jesus falls under his cross
VIII Jesus is helped by Simon of Cyrene
  IX Jesus meets the women of Jerusalem
   X Jesus is nailed to the cross
  XI Jesus speaks to his mother
 XII Jesus forgives the repentant thief
XIII Jesus dies on the cross
XIV Jesus is risen

These alterations in the traditional titles represent a changing attitude in what the Paschal Mystery means to us. During simplistic periods we were apparently only to have remorse because in some way our sins had made Jesus suffer that way. Supposedly we would be so filled with grief that we would go and sin no more. Now we are beginning to see these same events not as an historical oddity but as an ongoing process in which we are invited to participate. For example, the Brazilian theologian Leonardo Boffo, O.F.M., in *Way of the Cross—Way of Justice* (Orbis Books, 1980), accompanies each Station with a section labeled "Then" and one entitled

"Now" in which he ties the needs of today's struggling people with the cross of Jesus.

The Stations in This Book

The title *A Way of the Cross* is a recognition that there is no longer any single way to walk with Jesus. The community at Starcross Monastery has always maintained a practice of following the Stations. As our chapel is in the loft over the cow barn, there is not enough room to move physically from Station to Station. Instead we have selected a path along which we have placed fourteen simple markers. There has always been a preference for the Stations based on the Synoptic Gospels (Matthew, Mark and Luke). The selection of what is here Station II ("Jesus Prays in the Garden") to Station XII ("Jesus Is Buried") had evolved by Holy Week of 1980. At that time I was asked to give a short meditation on each Station during a retreat of high school students. That was the beginning of the "Reflections." After receiving information on the Clifton Stations we expanded our horizons. The final selection of Stations was made at the beginning of Lent 1983.

The desire was to frame the Way of the Cross in a Paschal and Eucharistic setting. As we did so we found a uniquely nourishing calling forth of both the anxieties and the hopes of our life experiences. Also, for the first time some of us realized at a deep level that the people of God could not have gone from the "Last Supper" to the breaking of bread at Emmaus without the intervening tragic journey to Golgotha. That is not to say that God could not have easily jumped from one to the other. But there is something basic in our human natures which lacks a full awareness of the presence of God within the Eucharist without the reality of the cross.

Some have observed a tendency in recent theology to shift from the cross to the resurrection as the focus of our salvation. The extreme of this at the popular level has led to a romantic spirituality which sees the cross and most of Jesus' life as simply a pre-condition for Easter. To those comfortably in that stance any Way of the Cross will have little attraction. However, there are also those today who with Karl Rahner are reflecting more closely on the death of Jesus, "not only in its redemptive effect, but also in itself . . . because it is called for by the reality itself." Those who see the cross as an important part of "God's self-utterance" are inclined to listen, and that is basically what lies behind the evolution of these Stations.

It is hoped that what is presented here will be seen within the larger framework of a post-Vatican II perspective. The Council helped us to reclaim the understanding that Christians and non-Christians alike are

> certainly bound to struggle with evil through many afflictions and to suffer death; but as one who has been made a partner in the Paschal Mystery and as one who has been configured to the death of Christ, he will go forward, strengthened by hope, to the resurrection (*Gaudium et Spes*, n. 22).

The Stations and Scripture

This book is not a study of Scripture but rather an evolution of a spiritual practice. Nonetheless, contemporary spirituality must always intersect with the profound contributions of today's scriptural scholars. Often the lessons are simple but require fundamental shifts in our thought patterns. We begin with the understanding that the Gospels are not biographies. The evangelists were making philosophical and theological statements for particular Christian communities. The Gospels do not present a consistent picture of Jesus. There are many differences and some conflicts between the various biblical accounts. To be understood properly each Gospel should be read separately. There is a danger of confusion where, as in this book, the accounts of the various evangelists are mixed together.

The Passion narratives are important keystones in each Gospel. Different images of Jesus are presented in these narratives. In Mark and Matthew it is emphasized that Jesus is the Son of God. As such he is obedient to God even to death. Although he will later come in glory, at the time of the Passion he is the suffering servant of God. His suffering is primarily the result of his being misunderstood and evidently abandoned. He stands silent and alone. Jesus has no support. He faces false witnesses and malevolent judges. His isolation culminates on the cross as he cries out the first words of Psalm 21/22, "My God, My God, why have you forsaken me?"

The community for which Mark was writing may have expected the imminent return of Jesus, but Matthew's community knew that it would take longer. Therefore, Matthew emphasizes the moral implications of following Jesus. Great care is taken to show that Jesus fulfilled the Scripture and a new covenant has been made between God and the people. The death of Jesus was the beginning of the final age. The Kingdom of God has been founded.

Luke focuses on God's plan for our salvation. Jesus is our gentle Savior, the instrument for healing and forgiveness. Luke's Gospel emphasizes that through encounter with God we will become whole once again. Even in the last few hours Jesus heals. At his arrest he cures the servant injured by a disciple (22:51). Peter was forgiven (22:32) even before he denied Jesus (22:54–62). Some have argued that he even healed the breach between Pilate and Herod (23:12). Jesus asked the women to be more concerned about their own future than his (23:28–32). As he was being crucified by the Romans he prayed, "Father, forgive them: they do not know what they are doing" (23:34). On the cross itself he was able to bring a criminal to salvation (23:43). The last words of Jesus in Luke's Gospel are not the anguished cry of the abandoned man as in Mark and Matthew. The desolation of Psalm 21/22 gives way to the more gentle Psalm 30/31 as Jesus cries out, "Father, into your hands I commit my spirit."

In John we find a triumphant and sovereign Jesus who has complete knowledge and control over the situation. At the end he says "It is accomplished" (19:30) and, seemingly of his own will, bows his head and gives up his spirit.

The different Gospel accounts arose out of the needs of the communities for whom they were written. Nonetheless, they echo traditions tied directly to Jesus. Today's communities, such as the one in which this Way of the Cross evolved, also have needs and make selections from the various Gospels as a link to that same source of our faith. The Gospel writers are not contestants for the "one truth." Rather they present facets of a truth which will always remain a mystery and can be given vitality only through the life experiences of generation after generation of Christians.

This book has a bias toward the humanism in Luke and away from the triumphalism in John. Yet Mark, not Luke, was selected for the Station of Jesus hanging on the cross. The alienation in our own age allows us to resonate with Mark's isolated Christ. Similarly, the resurrection story in John was used because it best describes, through Mary Magdalene, the spiritual hopes of the community first using these stations.

The episodes in all but two of the Stations are reflected in each of the Synoptic Gospels. However, some Gospels treat the particular events differently than others. There are major differences between the narrative of John and a number of the Stations.

Two Stations are mentioned only in Luke. Station VIII reflects on Jesus meeting the women as he carried his cross. Luke probably refers to a pious association who lamented over the condemned. This episode was selected to reflect the feminine presence in the Passion. There were three Stations with women in the traditional Way of the Cross. The other two, a meeting with Mary the mother of Jesus, and Veronica wiping his face, have no scriptural basis. All the evangelists mention women later in the narrative. Mark (15:40–42), Matthew (27:55–57) and Luke (23:49) have women watching the crucifixion. John places Jesus' mother near the cross with other women (19:25–27). The post-resurrection story in Station XIV is found in Luke, but other appearances are recorded in all the Gospels.

A Scripture scholar would have much more interest in the details of the trial of Jesus than is represented in Station IV. There is considerable study of the differences between the Gospels. Mark and Matthew have two meetings with the Sanhedrin, Luke has one, John has none. There is also great concern about the nature of the charges against Jesus. For the purposes of these stations the condemnation, rather than the accusations, is considered the bridge between our individual experience and the passion of Jesus.

Pictures

Under the old canonical regulations the important physical aspect of the Stations was not the picture but the little wooden cross on top of it. Many religious houses have only fourteen wooden crosses in their chapels. In general the simpler the image the more it can serve as a guide to our concentration. The more complicated an image becomes the more we are hindered from listening only to God speaking through our own inner experience. I was delighted to discover a photographic study by Sister Michael Marie Zobelein, who is noted for her treatment of contemplative subjects. She easily adapted and supplemented her art to conform to this text, thereby greatly enhancing the work.

Anyone who has walked the hills of coastal California has been attracted to the redwood fences which stand where they were erected in pioneer times. They were made from the heart of virgin redwoods and were probably living at the time our brother Jesus walked the earth. These posts provide the subject for the majority of the pictures in this book.

The continuing theme in all the pictures is wood. We are told that in a way wood never dies. Years after being milled it still responds to the environment. It was the last thing Our Lord touched. It was also a substance he knew well as a carpenter. For centuries on Good Friday the Christian community has shouted "Ecce lignum Crucis"—Behold the wood of the cross. In her pictures here Sister Michael Marie gives us the same invitation.

The Uses of This Book

The primary use of this work will probably be *personal*. An individual can sit and reflect on the great journey as part of his or her spiritual practice. Some may find it helpful to do this over a *fourteen day* period, using one Station each day.

In addition, many *small groups* may find this of some use in group meditation or worship. We have used it here at Starcross Monastery both in a physical outdoor pilgrimage as well as sitting in a circle in the chapel or the woods. This has been meaningful to the community and also used in *retreats* with a wide range of retreatants, including youth, families, and contemplatives, and, of course, especially at Holy Week.

Public worship is the traditional use of the Stations. Ecclesiastical authority has been required for alteration in the traditional scheme for public use. One advantage of simply erecting fourteen wooden crosses in a parish church is the opportunity to use various Ways of the Cross.

In any large group it would be well to have a *Leader* and a *Reader*. In a large congregation the Leader may travel with the Stations while the rest of the people remain at their places. It would be well for the Reader to remain at a lectern. There is, of course, no necessity for the Leader or Reader to be an ordained minister.

The normal formula used in the text could be

adapted to the functions of the Reader and Leader as follows:

1. Announcing the title of the Station (Leader)
2. Reading of the Scriptures (Reader)
3. Announcing the time of quiet (Leader)
4. Reading the reflection (Leader)
5. Announcing the time of quiet (Leader)
6. Responsory (Reader and Congregation)
7. Prayer (Leader)

There should be a slow and gentle rhythm in the whole experience, allowing time for quiet reflection before and after the devotions. It is here that we must allow God an opportunity to reach out to us.

The time required for either private or public use will probably be greater than is the normal practice.

In Memory

It would be inappropriate to make a dedication of a work like this. I have, however, been almost continually aware of the martyrs of our own times as I have written these words. Of those many saints, five have been uppermost in my mind.

Four of them were women in the struggle for justice. They were tortured, raped and murdered in El Salvador in 1980. Two were Maryknoll Sisters, one was an Ursuline Sister and one a lay volunteer.

Maura Clark, MM
1931–1980

Jean Donovan
1953–1980

Ita Ford, MM
1940–1980

Dorothy Kazel, OSU
1939–1980

The fifth was a Protestant theologian.

Dietrich Bonhoeffer
1906–1945

Pastor Bonhoeffer was hanged in an act of vicious revenge by a defeated dictator. The few works and the life of this martyr continue to lead both Protestants and Catholics to a greater degree of Christian discipleship.

Of your charity, my dear reader, you are asked to remember these and all the others who have followed our brother Jesus and who, in the words of Pastor Bonhoeffer, have taught us that "death is the supreme festival on the road to freedom."

Tolbert McCarroll
Starcross Monastery
Annapolis, Ca.

I Jesus Shares Supper with His Friends

For this is what I received from the Lord, and in turn passed on to you: that on the same night that he was betrayed, the Lord Jesus took some bread, and thanked God for it and broke it, and he said, "This is my body, which is for you; do this as a memorial of me." In the same way he took the cup after supper, and said, "This cup is the new covenant in my blood. Whenever you drink it, do this as a memorial of me."
1 Corinthians 11:23–25

A Quiet Moment

REFLECTION

A man came among us. He was gentle. He encouraged us and gave us hope. He did not condemn but reached out to the outcast. He brought peace where there had been strife and fear. He healed our bodies and our souls. He taught us to care for each other. He called us friends and showed us that we were all brothers and sisters of a loving Father. He invited us to walk with him.

Jesus was with us for such a short while. When the time was drawing near for him to leave us he gave us a great gift. He taught us how to be aware of his presence and to realize for all time the hope, peace and freedom we had experienced when he had walked together with us. For this great gift we have given thanks through the ages.

As Jews the disciples knew the importance of family life. The evening meal where the bread was broken and distributed was the important act of unity in the family. As the bread had been one, so was the family one. Yet many of Jesus' disciples were people without families for one reason or another. They were not able to experience that simple but deeply religious act when the head of the household breaks the bread and distributes it to all present.

Jesus reached out to all and said, "Anyone who does the will of my Father in heaven, he is my brother and sister and mother" (Mt 12:50). He became the host at the family table. He restored the communication between the dejected ones and God. Throughout his ministry he called us to a peaceful fellowship as he broke bread with us. Sometimes it was with throngs in the open air, and at other times it was in small intimate gatherings. With Jesus any meal became a divine experience never to be forgotten.

It is such a simple act to sit down and eat. How easy it is to take it for granted. But to a hungry person it is a special moment. How sweet it is to a person to share a meal with his loved ones after having been separated from them. For those who wander outside the Christian community the memory of the Eucharistic banquet is bittersweet. How happy they would be to stand at that holy table again. How healing is that first Communion after a long absence. Our brother has given us the food of the Kingdom but he left to us the responsibility for inviting the whole family to the table.

In the first years after Jesus left us our fathers and mothers prayed that as the different grains had been gathered from the hills and baked into one bread "so may your people be gathered from the ends of earth into your Kingdom" (The Didache). Today let it still be our prayer.

A Quiet Moment

RESPONSORY
Psalm 22/23

R. The Lord is my shepherd, there is nothing I shall want.

The Lord is my shepherd;
there is nothing I shall want.
Fresh and green are the pastures
where he gives me repose.
Near restful waters he leads me,
to revive my drooping spirit.

R. The Lord is my shepherd, there is nothing I shall want.

He guides me along the right path;
he is true to his name.

If I should walk in the valley of darkness
no evil would I fear.
You are there with your crook and your staff;
with these you give me comfort.

R. The Lord is my shepherd, there is nothing I shall want.

You have prepared a banquet for me
in the sight of my foes.
My head you have anointed with oil;
my cup is overflowing.

R. The Lord is my shepherd, there is nothing I shall want.

Surely goodness and kindness shall follow me
all the days of my life.
In the Lord's own house shall I dwell
for ever and ever.

R. The Lord is my shepherd, there is nothing I shall want.

PRAYER
Adapted from the Roman Missal

Gentle God, come live in your people
and strengthen us by your grace.
Help us to remain close to you in prayer
and give us a true love for one another.

R. *Amen.*

II *Jesus Prays in the Garden*

Then Jesus came with them to a small estate called Gethsemane; and he said to his disciples, "Stay here while I go over there to pray." He took Peter and the two sons of Zebedee with him. And sadness came over him, and great distress. Then he said to them, "My soul is sorrowful to the point of death. Wait here and keep awake with me." And going on a little further he fell on his face and prayed. "My Father," he said, "if it is possible, let this cup pass me by. Nevertheless, let it be as you, not I, would have it." He came back to the disciples and found them sleeping, and he said to Peter, "So you had not the strength to keep awake with me one hour? You should be awake, and praying not to be put to the test. The spirit is willing, but the flesh is weak." Again, a second time, he went away and prayed: "My Father," he said, "if this cup cannot pass by without my drinking it, your will be done!" And he came back again and found them sleeping, their eyes were so heavy. Leaving them there, he went away again and prayed for the third time, repeating the same words. Then he came back to the disciples and said to them, "You can sleep on now and take your rest. Now the hour has come when the Son of Man is to be betrayed into the hands of sinners. Get up! Let us go! My betrayer is already close at hand."

Matthew 26:36–46

A Quiet Moment

REFLECTION

The horrible end approaches. There is nothing to be done. Each victim of human cruelty feels completely alone. How much pleasure it gives us to take what is great and beautiful in this world and throw it into the mud. How exciting it is to violate others, to remove their freedom, to force them to conform to our own will.

Jesus was safe as long as he stayed out of Jerusalem and away from the political and religious games of his age. He could have ended his days as a wise old sage— the Buddah of Galilee. The game players would have been content with ignoring him and what he taught. But he did not take this path.

How many of our fellow humans at this very moment are crying out to God in their innermost hearts:

Do not hide your face from your servant;
answer quickly for I am in distress.

◆ ◆ ◆

I have reached the end of my strength.
I looked in vain for compassion,
for consolers; not one could I find.
Psalm 68/69

There is a solidarity between Jesus and all who have been abandoned. For our brother has also walked the depths of despair and entered the abyss of suffering. His agony can support those who stand up for what they must do, even when their friends do not understand them.

Let us seek forgiveness for those times when we left Jesus alone, when we fell asleep. When have we done this? There are times when we walked away from a brother or sister because we did not wish to be identified with them. There have been times when we could have reached out to a stranger in distress but we chose not to become involved. We have been ignorant of many things in this world of ours because we did not want to be aware of things which would disturb us. These are the times when we have left Jesus to suffer alone.

How very alone Jesus felt that night, and how very sad. But there is, as he knew, always hope.

A Quiet Moment

RESPONSORY
From Psalm 41/42

R. Hope in God; I will praise him still,
my savior and my God.

Deep is calling on deep,
in the roar of waters:
your torrents and all your waves
swept over me.

R. Hope in God; I will praise him still,
my savior and my God.

By day the Lord will send
his loving kindness;
by night I will sing to him,
praise the God of my life.

R. Hope in God; I will praise him still,
my savior and my God.

I will say to God, my rock:
'Why have you forgotten me?
Why do I go mourning
oppressed by the foe?'

R. Hope in God; I will praise him still,
my savior and my God.

With cries that pierce me to the heart,
my enemies revile me,
saying to me all the day long:
'Where is your God?'

R. Hope in God; I will praise him still,
my savior and my God.

Why are you cast down, my soul,
why groan within me?
Hope in God; I will praise him still,
my saviour and my God.

R. Hope in God; I will praise him still,
my savior and my God.

PRAYER
*Adapted from Dietrich Bonhoeffer's
prayer for his fellow prisoners*

O, God, help us to pray and to concentrate our thoughts on you. We cannot do this alone. In us there is darkness, but with you there is light. We are lonely, but you leave us not. We are feeble in heart, but with you there is peace. In us there is bitterness, but with you there is patience. We do not understand your ways, but you know the way for us. Help us, O God, through Jesus Christ our Lord.

R. *Amen.*

III
Jesus Is Betrayed and Disowned

He was still speaking when Judas, one of the Twelve, appeared, and with him a large number of men armed with swords and clubs, sent by the chief priests and elders of the people. Now the traitor had arranged a sign with them. "The one I kiss," he had said, "he is the man. Take him in charge." So he went straight up to Jesus and said, "Greetings, Rabbi," and kissed him. Jesus said to him, "My friend, do what you are here for." Then they came forward, seized Jesus and took him in charge. . . . Then all the disciples deserted him and ran away.

Meanwhile Peter was sitting outside in the courtyard, and a servant-girl came up to him and said, "You too were with Jesus the Galilean." But he denied it in front of them all. "I do not know what you are talking about," he said. When he went out to the gateway another servant girl saw him and said to the people there, "This man was with Jesus the Nazarene." And again, with an oath, he denied it. "I do not know the man." A little later the bystanders came up and said to Peter, "You are one of them for sure! Why, your accent gives you away." Then he started calling down curses on himself and swearing, "I do not know the man." At that moment the cock crew, and Peter remembered what Jesus had said, "Before the cock crows you will have disowned me three times." And he went outside and wept bitterly.

Matthew 26:47–50, 56, 69–75

A Quiet Moment

REFLECTION

From the day when he had entered the fresh and cool water of the Jordan River, Jesus had been surrounded by a loving community. Now he must suffer that special deep pain which only friends can inflict. He must face his ordeal alone, abandoned by the men and women who had been helped so much by his concern.

The peaceful world around Jesus has been shattered. The morality of the majority comes rushing to take possession of his life.

Rather than being seen as non-conformists, or considered different or odd, we also give in to the pressures around us. We are always reluctant to give up our security. On Sundays we claim to be one people. We wish each other the peace of God. On Mondays we deny each other. Those who have some privilege will not give up their advantage so that others may have a better life. When we do this we deny Jesus, for "I tell you solemnly, insofar as you neglected to do this to one of the least of these, you neglected to do it to me" (Mt 25:46).

When we see our brothers and sisters being unjustly deprived of their personhood in our communities we remain quiet and try not to become involved. We are especially prone to push aside the plight of those outsiders who are not part of our establishment. Paul, speaking for the spiritual rights of the Gentiles, had to confront the great Apostle Peter, the rock upon whom the Christian community was built. "I opposed him to his face, since he was manifestly in the wrong" (Galatians 2:11).

In a world badly in need of the peace of our brother Jesus, we are often called upon to confess his continued presence in history. How easy it is to remain silent rather than to be disapproved by our sophisticated friends. When we do so we also are saying, "I do not know the man."

A Quiet Moment

RESPONSORY
From Psalm 61/62

R. In God alone is my soul at rest.

How long will you all attack one man
to break him down,
as though he were a tottering wall,
or a tumbling fence?

R. In God alone is my soul at rest.

Their plan is only to destroy:
they take pleasure in lies.
With their mouth they utter blessing
but in their heart they curse.

R. In God alone is my soul at rest.

In God alone be at rest, my soul;
for my hope comes from him.
He alone is my rock, my stronghold,
my fortress: I stand firm.

R. In God alone is my soul at rest.

PRAYER

    Gentle God, give us the courage to make justice a living thing in our hearts. Show us the world as it is where our brothers and sisters are struggling the same as we. Turn us from every comfortable false reality and deliver us from spiritual romanticism. Help us to accept and to appreciate the seasons of the harsh wind, and guide us to reconquer that destiny which you have already given us.
    Where we cannot rid the world of evil, help us to each personally reduce the evil in our own corner of existence. Help us to confront what must be confronted, but without hatred for one another. Support those who have better vision and more courage than the rest of us, and guide them in the dark moments of their lonely journey. Shelter us all in your peace.

R. *Amen.*

IV *Jesus Is Condemned*

They began their accusation by saying, "We found this man inciting our people to revolt, opposing payment of the tribute to Caesar, and claiming to be Christ, a king." Pilate put to him this question, "Are you the king of the Jews?" "It is you who say it," he replied. Pilate then said to the chief priests and the crowd, "I find no case against this man." But they persisted, "He is inflaming the people with his teaching all over Judaea; it has come all the way from Galilee, where he started, down to here." When Pilate heard this, he asked if the man were a Galilean; and finding that he came under Herod's jurisdiction he passed him over to Herod who was also in Jerusalem at that time.

Herod was delighted to see Jesus; he had heard about him and had been wanting for a long time to set eyes on him; moreover, he was hoping to see some miracle worked by him. So he questioned him at some length, but without getting any reply. Meanwhile the chief priests and the scribes were there, violently pressing their accusations. Then Herod, together with his guards, treated him with contempt and made fun of him; he put a rich cloak on him and sent him back to Pilate. And though Herod and Pilate had been enemies before, they were reconciled that same day.

Pilate then summoned the chief priests and the leading men and the people. "You brought this man before me," he said, "as a political agitator. Now I have gone into the matter myself in your presence and found no case against the man in respect of all the charges you bring against him. Nor has Herod either, since he has sent him back to us. As you can see, the man has done nothing that deserves death, so I shall have him flogged and then let him go." But as one man they howled, "Away with him! Give us Barabbas!" (This man had been thrown into prison for causing a riot in the city and for murder.)

Pilate was anxious to see Jesus free and addressed them again, but they shouted back, "Crucify him! Crucify him!" And for the third time he spoke to them, "Why? What harm has this man done? I have found no case against him that deserves death, so I shall have him punished and then let him go." But they kept on shouting at the top of their voices, demanding that he should be crucified. And their shouts were growing louder.

Pilate then gave his verdict: their demand was to be granted.

Luke 23:2–24

A Quiet Moment

REFLECTION

Standing alone and silent, Jesus hears the dread words from this stranger who now controls his life. He is to die, to suffer and to die. In a few hours his life will be no more. There will be no more walks on the green hills, no more listening to the sound of the waves, no more smiles of friends, no more quiet moments by the fire. All that is left is pain and death.

> Joy has vanished from our hearts:
> our dancing has turned to mourning.
> *Lamentations 5:15*

Jesus was a threat to Rome. He was not a big threat, but a threat. He might cause a disturbance. This odd Jew was a nuisance to the law and order of society. He must be shut up and made an example. Little bureaucrats of church and state play their age-old games, grinding up the souls of the innocent.

Let us learn from Jesus' example how to be pure in the unjust fights of life. Let him teach us the language of silence that cuts through the noise of the centuries.

> Harshly dealt with, he bore it humbly,
> he never opened his mouth,
> like a lamb that is led to the slaughter-house,
> like a sheep that is dumb before its shearers
> never opening its mouth.
> *Isaiah 53:7*

How often are we like Pilate, ready to smash anyone who gets in our way, who threatens our position, our popularity, our enjoyment. In such times we look for a scapegoat. We must have someone to blame for our inconvenience.

Jesus insisted on being a free person. He ignored the artificialities of the establishment. Furthermore, he announced the coming of the Kingdom. He invited the poor and the outcasts to be as happy as the privileged classes. This was wonderful for the little people. But it made the great ones uncomfortable. People do not like to be irritated. They will strike out at the source of the irritation.

But there was more. Jesus showed that he knew God. He announced that the Father was no mysterious hidden King; he was a warm and caring "Abba"—a Dad who freely acknowledges that he belongs to us and we to him. This was called a blasphemy, an unforgivable indignity to God. Only the authorized leaders were credentialed to announce God's will and law.

For these disturbances to the comfortableness of society, Jesus must die and be shown up for what he is—a nothing. He will die the humiliating death reserved for the lowest of creatures. Through the centuries countless men and women have been removed from the sunlight in one way or another because they dared to be themselves and ignored the rules of the game. Yet their silent suffering has often contributed greatly to the unfolding of life in future ages.

A Quiet Moment

RESPONSORY
From Psalm 40/41

R. Blessed be the Lord, the God of Israel
from age to age. Amen. Amen.

Happy the man
who considers the poor and the weak.
The Lord will save him in the day of evil,
will guard him, give him life,
make him happy in the land
and will not give him up to the will of his foes.

R. Blessed be the Lord, the God of Israel
from age to age. Amen. Amen.

My enemies whisper against me.
They all weigh up the evil which is on me:
'Some deadly thing has fastened upon him,
he will not rise again from where he lies.'

R. Blessed be the Lord, the God of Israel
from age to age. Amen. Amen.

Thus even my friend, in whom I trusted,
who ate my bread, has turned against me.
But you, O Lord, have mercy on me.
If you uphold me I shall be unharmed
and set in your presence for evermore.

R. Blessed be the Lord, the God of Israel
from age to age. Amen. Amen.

PRAYER
From the Book of Common Prayer

O God, whose Son forgave his enemies while he was suffering shame and death: Strengthen those who suffer for the sake of conscience; when they are accused, save them from speaking in hate; when they are rejected, save them from bitterness; when they are imprisoned, save them from despair; and to us your servants, give grace to respect their witness and to discern the truth, that our society may be cleansed and strengthened. This we ask for the sake of Jesus Christ, our merciful and righteous judge.

R. *Amen.*

V *Jesus Is Tortured*

Then he released Barabbas for them. He ordered Jesus to be first scourged and then handed over to be crucified.

The governor's soldiers took Jesus with them into the praetorium and collected the whole cohort around him. Then they stripped him and made him wear a scarlet cloak, and having twisted some thorns into a crown they put this on his head and placed a reed in his right hand. To make fun of him they knelt to him saying, "Hail, king of the Jews!"

Matthew 27:26–29

A Quiet Moment

REFLECTION

How we would like to skip over what happened at the hands of the Roman soldiers. What is happening to the sweet and gentle Jesus who gathered around him all who were sick in body and soul, who stood upon the mountain and said, "Blessed are the peacemakers, for they shall be called the children of God"? This same Jesus was stripped naked before brutal soldiers who wanted to see him in agony.

> For my part, I made no resistance,
> neither did I turn away.
> I offered my back to those who struck me
> my cheek to those who tore at my beard;
> I did not cover my face
> against insult and spittle.
>
> *Isaiah 50:6*

Tied to a post he awaited the first lash. Hours before he had sat serenely surrounded by his friends in the still of the evening. They broke bread and knew that God was with them. Now he was alone, only an object to the soldiers. The first blow cut deep, and then came one after another, for this was really how the Romans killed their enemies. They were whipped almost to death. Then their near dead bodies were hung on a cross as an example to all the enemies of Rome. Methodically the blows fell. His flesh ran with blood. Welts and bruises appeared. We like to think that he was silent, but he could not have been. It was not possible. The soldiers would have gotten their satisfaction. He would have screamed. He could not have helped it. And, he would have passed out. But the blows would have continued until there was little life left.

Revived enough to walk, the crown of thorns was pressed down upon that innocent head. Then his clothes were thrown over him again. It was time to get on with it. They dragged him away, half dead.

> As the crowds were appalled on seeing him
> —so disfigured did he look
> that he seemed no longer human—
>
> *Isaiah 52:14*

When he experienced this torture Jesus became a part of the suffering of all the victims of violence throughout history. There are people whose whole life is one long crucifixion because of the dehumanized existence forced upon them. Every day some of our brothers and sisters are subject to violent barbarities. Jesus is there with them offering help and strength out of his own suffering.

There are times when what was meant to be a brutal degradation becomes a heroic moment. The force that was meant to destroy can, with God's help, be transformed into a new life.

A Quiet Moment

RESPONSORY
From Psalm 118/119 vv. 41–48

R. Lord, let your love come upon me,
the saving help of your promise.

And I shall answer those who taunt me
for I trust in your word.
Do not take the word of truth from my mouth
for I trust in your decrees.

R. Lord, let your love come upon me,
the saving help of your promise.

I shall always keep your law
for ever and ever.
I shall walk in the path of freedom
for I seek your precepts.
I will speak of your will before kings
and not be abashed.

R. Lord, let your love come upon me,
the saving help of your promise.

Your commands have been my delight;
these I have loved.
I will worship your commands and love them
and ponder your statutes.

R. Lord, let your love come upon me,
the saving help of your promise.

PRAYER

O God, help us to meet you in the sufferings of our brothers and sisters. We were not there to comfort your Son in that dread hour. We pray for the courage to be with him now, wherever the lash will strike again. Protect us from ever being the instruments of pain for any of your children.

R. *Amen.*

VI *Jesus Carries His Cross*

They then took charge of Jesus, and carrying his own cross he went out of the city to the place of the skull or, as it was called in Hebrew, Golgotha.

John 19:17

A Quiet Moment

REFLECTION

Rome was cruel to rebels. Crucifixion was a form of public humiliation. Death was slow and painful.

Always efficient, it was considered practical by the Romans for the prisoner to carry the cross beam of his cross. This was tied to the back of the condemned man. There were many crucifixions those days, and the vertical timbers were simply left in place. The poor unfortunate man was nailed naked to the cross piece and hauled up by ropes. Then his feet were nailed to the vertical timber.

With Jesus the soldiers had done their job well. He was weak from the beating. Still, he was made to enter the jeering crowd, stumbling along with the heavy timber. He was in the company of two criminals who were to suffer the same fate.

It is doubtful that he noticed the faces of the crowd. If he had any earthly thought it was probably for the pain he was suffering. There actually would not have been many in the crowd with hatred in their eyes. Most would be happy and laughing. Everyone was in a holiday spirit. The Passion of Jesus was just one of the side-shows for country people coming into the big city of Jerusalem at this festive time. In fact for some it must have been sport to see the soldiers prodding the prisoners along. Some would have even joined in the fun, thrown the last part of a loaf of bread or melon at the prisoners and laughed at their startled reaction. After all, everyone knew that people condemned to death were bad people and fair game. Most of the crowd would have passed on after a few minutes to see the other marvels of the city.

A few people would follow Jesus as they had followed him for years over the beautiful hills of Galilee. Later the early Christians were to sing:

> His state was divine,
> yet he did not cling
> to his equality with God
> but emptied himself
> to assume the condition of a slave,
> and became as men are;
> and being as all men are,
> he was humbler yet,
> even to accepting death,
> death on a cross.

But for now the majesty was gone and there was only the pain.

Around us at this moment are also people in great

pain. There are people at this instant whose world has collapsed. Hope has gone from them. Inwardly they cry out and scratch desperately at the walls of the pit into which they have fallen. Yet we pass them by with hardly a glance. If they are seen at all they are only an inconvenience, a disturbance to us. We, like the holiday crowd in Jerusalem those many years ago, move on to more pleasant things.

A Quiet Moment

RESPONSORY
From Psalm 118/119 vv. 81–88

R. I yearn for your saving help.
I hope in your word.

My eyes yearn to see your promise.
When will you console me?
Though parched and exhausted with waiting
I remember your statutes.

R. I yearn for your saving help.
I hope in your word.

How long must your servant suffer?
When will you judge my foes?
For me the proud have dug pitfalls,
against your law.

R. I yearn for your saving help.
   I hope in your word.

   Your commands are all true; then help me
   when lies oppress me.
   They almost made an end of me on earth
   but I kept your precepts.
   Because of your love give me life
   and I will do your will.

R. I yearn for your saving help.
   I hope in your word.

PRAYER

Gentle God, help us to be aware of each other's cares. Give us the grace to see beyond ourselves. As your Son endured the hardship of this last journey, let us be patient with each other. Help us to support one another on our own pilgrimages in life. Give us the courage to share the burden of each other's crosses and to follow in our brother's footsteps.

R. *Amen.*

VII
Jesus Is Helped by Simon of Cyrene

They led him out to crucify him. They enlisted a passer-by, Simon of Cyrene, father of Alexander and Rufus, who was coming in from the country, to carry his cross. They brought Jesus to the place called Golgotha, which means the place of the skull.

Mark 15:21–22

A Quiet Moment

REFLECTION

If they were ever to get Jesus up to the place of execution they would have to get someone else to carry that timber. Jesus simply could not make it. They drafted a man out of the crowd, but they may have been outwitted. For this man they grabbed may have put himself where he could have been chosen. His sons, we are told, were known to the early Christians. And perhaps it was his wife who was later to befriend the Apostle Paul. Perhaps Simon had even taunted the soldiers about how slowly everything was going, until in frustration one of them said, "All right, then, you carry it."

Let us construct a picture of Simon in our imagination. Perhaps he was a simple man. He may have listened but only half understood the discussions between his sons and their intellectual friends as they related the significance of Jesus in history. Perhaps Simon was not even sure he was a follower of Jesus. Yet he had the courage to be there when others fled. He could well understand the needs of a man in deep trouble. He knew what to do and he did it. Now, carrying the cross, Simon was at home. He had a task to perform and he was doing it. The cross was heavy but his shoulders were used to work. This was no time to think; it was a time to work. It was only later that he would realize that like all the leaders of the Christian community he too had walked with Jesus.

It is probable that Jesus did not even know what was happening at this point, but once the impossible weight of the timber was lifted from him he could focus his remaining energy on what was to come. Jesus always welcomed the help of very ordinary people, beginning with that other Simon, Peter. Now this strong man from North Africa was performing a great service. For Jesus was not yet to be crushed in the crowded streets of Jerusalem. He could muster the dignity he needed to convert this atrocity into the great spiritual act of the ages. If Simon were known to Jesus, then he would have known that he was not alone at this awful moment.

What is there in us that allows us to ignore someone else's pain and sorrow, and sometimes even to feel good about it? Is it that we are relieved we ourselves are not in trouble? Or do we not want to be associated with the victim for fear the crowd, or fate, will turn on us as well? All of Jesus' close friends and his learned associates were not there. Simon, the simple fellow from faraway Cyrene, was there when he was needed.

In ordinary times Church people use all the right words and we convince ourselves that we are truly God's people. But when difficulties appear our words are often without substance. When the moment of truth comes we are too often interested in our religion because of worldly reasons—power, prestige, security, emotional well-being. More than we realize, the cross of Jesus has been borne by those who did not know him well, or at all. We, his brothers and sisters, often stand and watch comfortably from the sidelines.

A Quiet Moment

RESPONSORY
From Psalm 145/146

R. He is happy who is helped by the Lord our God.

My soul, give praise to the Lord;
I will praise the Lord all my days,
make music to my God while I live.

R. He is happy who is helped by the Lord our God.

Put no trust in princes,
in mortal men in whom there is no help.
Take their breath, they return to clay
and their plans that day come to nothing.

R. He is happy who is helped by the Lord our God.

> He is happy who is helped by Jacob's God,
> whose hope is in the Lord his God,
> who alone made heaven and earth,
> the seas and all they contain.

R. He is happy who is helped by the Lord our God.

> It is he who keeps faith for ever,
> who is just to those who are oppressed.
> It is he who gives bread to the hungry,
> the Lord, who sets prisoners free.

R. He is happy who is helped by the Lord our God.

> The Lord who gives sight to the blind,
> who raises up those who are bowed down,
> the Lord, who protects the stranger
> and upholds the widow and orphan.

R. He is happy who is helped by the Lord our God.

> It is the Lord who loves the just
> but thwarts the path of the wicked.
> The Lord will reign for ever,
> Zion's God, from age to age.

R. He is happy who is helped by the Lord our God.

PRAYER
Suggested by a poem of Dietrich Bonhoeffer written in prison July 18, 1944

Lord, help us to be here when you need us. Teach us to be useful when you are under a wicked weight. Let us find you among the poor and the scorned, where there is no shelter or bread. We want to stand by you in your hour of grieving. Give us the courage to dirty our hands in the ordinary needs of your people. Show us the way, dear Lord.

R. *Amen.*

VIII
Jesus Meets the Women

Large numbers of people followed him, and of women too, who mourned and lamented for him. But Jesus turned to them and said, "Daughters of Jerusalem, do not weep for me; weep rather for yourselves and for your children. For the days will surely come when people will say, 'Happy are those who are barren, the wombs that have never borne, the breasts that have never suckled!' Then they will begin to *say to the mountains, 'Fall on us!'; to the hill, 'Cover us!'* For if men use the green wood like this, what will happen when it is dry?"

Luke 23:27–32

A Quiet Moment

REFLECTION

It is not surprising that Jesus would meet women on the way to his death. Then, as now, they would have constituted more than half of the population. Furthermore, it is at times of spiritual crisis that women provide the strength of any community. There is no mystery about that. A woman has a greater tolerance for uncertainty, because she has been conditioned to exist despite the arbitrary decisions made by her father, pastor, employer, husband, or son. When the whole world turns upside-down a man will not easily give up his expectations of controlling his destiny. The woman, however, is on familiar ground.

Jesus was a good friend to women:

> Now after this he made his way through towns and villages preaching, and proclaiming the Good News of the kingdom of God. With him went the Twelve, as well as certain women who had been cured of evil spirits and ailments: Mary surnamed the Magdalene, from whom seven demons had gone out, Joanna the wife of Herod's steward Chuza, Susanna, and several others who provided for them out of their own resources.
>
> *Luke 8:1–3*

It was a characteristic of his ministry, of what it meant to be in the Christian community, that women were treated more fairly than in the surrounding culture. Once again Jesus spoke as an equal to women. He refused to be an object of pity, for he was the subject of salvation. He had a dire warning to give. The tears of the women were nothing compared with what was to come. Was he only predicting the bloody fall of Jerusalem in a few years? Can we not also hear this as speaking to the women of the world, as yet unborn?

The woman who has become the victim of violence is very close to the passion of Jesus. How routine it has become to degrade and humiliate feminine victims. Soldiers feel it is their right to plunder the dignity and the personhood of any woman they find. The battlefield can be anyplace from the jungles of Latin America to the streets of large cities, and even into the homes of middle class America.

Yet in this final journey, despite all fear for personal harm, were the women of Jesus' life—his mother, his friends like Mary Magdalene and many others to whom he gave hope and health. With his help they had blossomed with openness and a readiness to accept the good gifts of life. Yet here on the way to Golgotha they are the symbol of suffering. So it was then and so it is today in our own streets of tears.

A Quiet Moment

RESPONSORY
From Psalm 136/137

R. Remember us, O Lord.

> By the rivers of Babylon
> there we sat and wept,
> remembering Zion;
> on the poplars that grew there
> we hung up our harps.

R. Remember us, O Lord.

> For it was there that they asked us,
> our captors, for songs,

our oppressors, for joy.
'Sing to us,' they said,
'one of Zion's songs.'

R. Remember us, O Lord.

O how could we sing
the song of the Lord
on alien soil?
If I forget you, Jerusalem,
let my right hand wither!

R. Remember us, O Lord.

PRAYER
Suggested by the Tao Te Ching

God, show us how to assist you in giving life to all, to help us develop our individual natures and to give to each an inner strength. Give us the grace to nourish people without claiming authority over them, to benefit them without demanding gratitude, to guide them without seeking to control them. Help us, Lord, to blunt our sharpness and to soften our glare. Give us freedom from our selfish concerns and let us join you and all our sisters and brothers in a partnership of living.

R. *Amen.*

IX
Jesus Is Nailed to the Cross

When they had reached the place called Golgotha, that is, the place of the skull, they gave him wine to drink mixed with gall, which he tasted but refused to drink. When they had finished crucifying him they shared out his clothing by casting lots, and then sat down and stayed there keeping guard over him.

Above his head was placed the charge against him; it read: "This is Jesus, the King of the Jews."

Matthew 27:33–37

A Quiet Moment

REFLECTION

The Romans were efficient in all things, even the execution of slaves and criminals of the lowest class. For them they used the cruelest form of death by torture—crucifixion. It was also used for political insurgents, which is probably how they classified Jesus.

He was stripped naked. Rough hands held his arms as the long spikes were driven through his wrists. He was hauled up, his flesh torn apart and his brain exploding with the pain. His ankles were nailed down. His young body was now completely violated. All that remained was to wait for him to die, from the vicious whipping, exhaustion, and thirst.

Everything that was his was taken away. On the cross he had nothing. Naked he was when he came into this world, the first son of good and simple people, with whom he walked the green hills of Galilee. He had learned to feel the presence of God, and to warm to the security of the earth and its creatures. Naked he was when but a few years ago he was baptized in the Jordan River and accepted his divine calling. Naked he was again before the world on this cross of shame. He was completely powerless, unable to remove even one of the hordes of insects that crawled over the open wounds of his body or to hide anything from the eyes of those who passed by.

We find many excuses to take life. We can act as if the victim is not human, only a yet to be born child, a criminal, a political or social undesirable, or an enemy in war. Sometimes we attempt to be humane in our murder, but at other times we intentionally or thoughtlessly inflict great pain out of vengeance and a desire for revenge.

It is the obligation of the brothers and sisters of Jesus not only to avoid anything which debases a fellow human being and to seek clemency and mercy for those condemned to death; we must also, in memory of our crucified brother, become the voice for the voiceless in our society.

A Quiet Moment

RESPONSORY
From Psalm 68/69

R. Save me, O God.

    Save me, O God,
    for the waters have risen to my neck.
    I have sunk into the mud of the deep
    and there is no foothold.
    I have entered the waters of the deep
    and the waves overwhelm me.

R. Save me, O God.

    I am wearied with all my crying,
    my throat is parched.
    My eyes are wasted away
    from looking for my God.

R. Save me, O God.

    Lord, answer, for your love is kind;
    in your compassion, turn towards me.
    Do not hide your face from your servant;
    answer quickly for I am in distress.
    Come close to my soul and redeem me;
    ransom me pressed by my foes.

R. Save me, O God.

You know how they taunt and deride me;
my oppressors are all before you.
Taunts have broken my heart;
I have reached the end of my strength.
I looked in vain for compassion,
for consolers; not one could I find.
For food they gave me poison;
in my thirst they gave me vinegar to drink.

R. Save me, O God.

PRAYER
Suggested by the writings of St. Augustine

Father, we pray on behalf of those who cannot reach out to you at this moment. Protect those who are facing adversity. Strengthen those who need courage. Keep watch over those who weep. Tend the sick, give rest to the weary, bless the dying, soothe the suffering. Please, dear Lord, let the victims of cruelty and oppression know that you are with them at this moment.

R. *Amen.*

X   *Jesus Hangs on the Cross*

And they crucified two robbers with him, one on his right and one on his left.

The passers-by jeered at him; they shook their heads and said, "Aha! So you would destroy the Temple and rebuild it in three days! Then save yourself: come down from the cross!" The chief priests and the scribes mocked him among themselves in the same way. "He saved others," they said; "he cannot save himself. Let the Christ, the king of Israel, come down from the cross now, for us to see it and believe." Even those who were crucified with him taunted him.

When the sixth hour came there was darkness over the whole land until the ninth hour. And at the ninth hour Jesus cried out in a loud voice, "Eloi, Eloi lama sabachthani?" which means, *My God, my God, why have you deserted me?"*

Mark 15:27–34

A Quiet Moment

REFLECTION

Now Jesus hangs on the cross between heaven and earth. The pain has dulled. All feeling is gradually leaving his body. His time is short. He prays. He raises his voice to God in the words of the Psalm:

> My God, my God, why have you forsaken me?
> You are far from my plea
> and the cry of my distress.
> O my God, I call by day and you give no reply;
> I call by night and I find no peace.
>
> Yet you, O God, are holy,
> enthroned on the praises of Israel.
> In you our fathers put their trust;
> they trusted and you set them free.
> When they cried to you, they escaped.
> In you they trusted and never in vain.
>
> But I am a worm and no man,
> the butt of men, laughing-stock of the people.
> All who see me deride me.
> They curl their lips, they toss their heads.
> "He trusted in the Lord; let him save him;
> let him release him if this is his friend."
>
> Yes, it was you who took me from the womb,
> entrusted me to my mother's breast.
> To you I was committed from my birth,
> from my mother's womb you have been my God.
> Do not leave me alone in my distress;
> come close, there is none else to help.
>
> Many bulls have surrounded me,
> fierce bulls of Bashan close me in.
> Against me they open wide their jaws,
> like lions, rending and roaring.

Like water I am poured out,
disjointed are all my bones.
My heart has become like wax,
it is melted within my breast.

Parched as burnt clay is my throat,
my tongue cleaves to my jaws.

Many dogs have surrounded me,
a band of the wicked beset me.
They tear holes in my hands and my feet
and lay me in the dust of death.

I can count every one of my bones.
These people stare at me and gloat;
they divide my clothing among them.
They cast lots for my robe.
Psalm 21/22

Those around the cross are quiet now. The crowd has thinned out. The scoffers are silent and begin to move away. Around the cross a deep stillness has descended and touches the hearts of those few who watch. Now, at last, some people are beginning to awaken.

A Quiet Moment

RESPONSORY
From Psalm 50/51

R. Have mercy on me, God, in your kindness.

Have mercy on me, God, in your kindness.
In your compassion blot out my offense.
O wash me more and more from my guilt
and cleanse me from my sin.

R. Have mercy on me, God, in your kindness.

My offenses truly I know them;
my sin is always before me.
Against you, you alone, have I sinned;
what is evil in your sight I have done.

R. Have mercy on me, God, in your kindness.

Indeed you love truth in the heart;
then in the secret of my heart teach me wisdom.
O purify me, then I shall be clean;
O wash me, I shall be whiter than snow.

R. Have mercy on me, God, in your kindness.

A pure heart create for me, O God,
put a steadfast spirit within me.

Do not cast me away from your presence,
nor deprive me of your holy spirit.

R. Have mercy on me, God, in your kindness.

PRAYER
Suggested by the writings of Thomas Traherne

Gentle God, help us to understand the cross as the abyss of wonders, the center of desires, the school of virtues, the house of wisdom, the throne of love, the creator of joy, and the place of sorrows. Let us comprehend it as the root of happiness and the gate of heaven.

R. *Amen.*

XI   *Jesus Dies*

. . . But Jesus gave a loud cry and breathed his last. And the veil of the Temple was torn in two from top to bottom. The centurion, who was standing in front of him, had seen how he had died, and he said, "In truth this man was a son of God."

There were some women watching from a distance. Among them were Mary of Magdala, Mary who was the mother of James the younger and Joses, and Salome. These used to follow him and look after him when he was in Galilee. And there were many other women there who had come up to Jerusalem with him.

Mark 15:37–41

A Quiet Moment

REFLECTION

Now it is over. The wise one is dead. In the Book of Wisdom it is written:

Let us lie in wait for the virtuous man,
since he annoys us and opposes our way of life,
reproaches us for our breaches of the law
and accuses us of playing false to our upbringing.

He claims to have knowledge of God,
and calls himself a son of the Lord.
Before us he stands,
a reproof to our way of thinking,
the very sight of him weighs our spirits down;
his way of life is not like other men's,
the paths he treads are unfamiliar.
In his opinion we are counterfeit;
he holds aloof from our doings
as though from filth;
he proclaims the final end
of the virtuous as happy
and boasts of having God for his father.
Let us see if what he says is true,
let us observe what kind of end
he himself will have.
If the virtuous man is God's son,
God will take his part
and rescue him from the clutches of his enemies.
Let us test him with cruelty and with torture,
and thus explore this gentleness of his
and put his endurance to the proof.
Let us condemn him to a shameful death
since he will be looked after—
we have his word for it.

Wisdom 2:12–20

What a strange image for the world, a crucified sage. Yet, out of this hour will come a new hope for the human race. The cross, the symbol of shame, will become a sign of glory. From these few friends watching this event will grow a great fellowship which will last through the centuries. No one will ever truly know what happened. But with the centurion we can say, "In truth this man was a son of God."

There have been many other brothers and sisters of Jesus who have also suffered through the ages because their way of life was not like other people's. Like him they held aloof from corruption and were oppressed because their lives were a reproach to us for being false to what we could become.

For our brother Jesus the lonely agony ended on that hill outside of Jerusalem. Let us join the women who watched and prayed in silence. Let us pray not only for ourselves but also on behalf of those innocent ones who are suffering at this moment. Let us approach the cross in solidarity with Jesus and with the victims of cruelty in our own age.

V. This is the wood of the cross,
on which hung the salvation of the world;

R. Come, let us worship.

A Time of Stillness and Silent Prayer

R. *Amen.*

XII Jesus Is Buried

Then a member of the council arrived, an upright and virtuous man named Joseph. He had not consented to what the others had planned and carried out. He came from Arimathea, a Jewish town, and he lived in the hope of seeing the Kingdom of God. This man went to Pilate and asked for the body of Jesus. He then took it down, wrapped it in a shroud and put him in a tomb which was hewn in stone in which no one had yet been laid. It was Preparation Day and the sabbath was imminent.

Meanwhile the women who had come from Galilee with Jesus were following behind. They took note of the tomb and of the position of the body.

Then they returned and prepared spices and ointments. And on the sabbath day they rested, as the Law required.

Luke 23:50–56

A Quiet Moment

REFLECTION

Today we look back through the centuries to that day when our brother was killed. Most other great religious leaders have died happy, peaceful deaths. Jesus' death seemed to say that the details of death are unimportant. The quality of our lives is what is important.

We say that Jesus is our Savior. From what does he save us? He liberates us from meaningless and useless lives; from the hopelessness that comes from being powerless to change the world; from the soul sickness that comes from participating in a mechanical society greedily seeking its fulfillment in pleasure. He has the answer for the question, "Is there nothing else to life?" He offers to help us put aside the false faces we wear and to learn who we are. By his life and death he encourages us to believe that love is possible, that hurts can be healed.

Death is becoming once again unborn. The turbulent strivings of our individual lives merge into a river of peace. But this deep tranquility need not be postponed to the end of life. We are daily invited to leave our busyness for a while. The Way of the Cross we are walking together helps us to understand that there is, indeed, something else in life. Now, with our brother Jesus, let us rest for a moment in God's holy and refreshing stillness.

A Quiet Moment

RESPONSORY
From Luke 1:68–79

R. Blessed be the Lord, the God of Israel.
   He has visited his people and redeemed them.

He has raised up for us a mighty saviour
in the house of David his servant
as he promised by the lips of holy men
those who were his prophets from of old.

R. Blessed be the Lord, the God of Israel.
He has visited his people and redeemed them.

A saviour who would free us from our foes,
from the hands of all who hate us
so his love for our fathers is fulfilled
and his holy covenant remembered.

R. Blessed be the Lord, the God of Israel.
He has visited his people and redeemed them.

To make known to his people their salvation,
through forgiveness of all their sins
the loving kindness of the heart of our God
who visits us like dawn from on high.

R. Blessed be the Lord, the God of Israel.
He has visited his people and redeemed them.

He will give light to those in darkness,
those who dwell in the shadow of death,
and guide us into the way of peace.

R. Blessed be the Lord, the God of Israel.
He has visited his people and redeemed them.

PRAYER

O Gentle One, you are our trust, the stillness in whom there is no change. Call us home from wherever we may have wandered. Help us to discard the memories of our busyness that in simplicity we may rediscover the wonder of your way. Heal our hurt and protect our joy. Guide us to the peace of your presence and help us to find rest in the warmth of your love.

R. *Amen.*

XIII   *Jesus Is Risen!*

It was very early on the first day of the week, and still dark, when Mary of Magdala came to the tomb. She saw that the stone had been moved away from the tomb and came running to Simon Peter and the other disciple, the one Jesus loved. "They have taken the Lord out of the tomb," she said, "and we don't know where they have put him."

So Peter set out with the other disciple to go to the tomb. They ran together, but the other disciple, running faster than Peter, reached the tomb first; he bent down and saw the linen cloths lying on the ground, but did not go in. Simon Peter who was following now came up, went right into the tomb, saw the linen cloths on the ground, and also the cloth that had been over his head; this was not with the linen cloths but rolled up in a place by itself. Then the other disciple who had reached the tomb first also went in; he saw and he believed. Till this moment they had failed to understand the teaching of scripture, that he must rise from the dead. The disciples then went home again.

Meanwhile Mary stayed outside near the tomb, weeping. Then, still weeping, she stooped to look inside, and saw two angels in white sitting where the body of Jesus had been, one at the head, the other at the feet. They said, "Woman, why are you weeping?" "They have taken my Lord away," she replied, "and I don't know where they have put him." As she said this she turned around and saw Jesus standing there, though she did not recognize him. Jesus said, "Woman, why are you weeping? Whom are you looking for?" Supposing him to be the gardener, she said, "Sir, if you have taken him away, tell me where you have put him, and I will go and remove him." Jesus said, "Mary!" She knew him then and said to him in Hebrew, "Rabbuni!"—which means Master. Jesus said to her, "Do not cling to me, because I have not yet ascended to the Father. But go and find the brothers, and tell them: I am ascending to my Father and your Father, to my God and your God."

John 20:1–17

A Quiet Moment

REFLECTION

"Beneath happiness crouches misery, on misery perches happiness" advises the ancient Chinese sage. Over and apart from the great religious significance of these events there were the little human tragedies of those who needed Jesus. One of these was Miriam, of the town known as Magdala or Magadan. She has become known to us by the Greek "Mary Magdalene" or sometimes more simply by the French term "La Madeleine."

She had lived in Galilee in a town on the edge of the plain of Gennesaret on the west shore of the beautiful Sea of Galilee. The town was on the important caravan route between Nazareth and Damascus. We do not know when she first met Jesus. It was near here that he fed the multitude and where he would put out in a boat to find rest. Perhaps it was at one of these times he found someone else who desperately needed rest. Miriam was filled with inner torment, with "seven demons" (Lk 8:2). Her town was known for its wealth and its corrupt morals. In some way she had become trapped in the snares of worldly life. There seemed no exit to her private hell and she lived without hope—until she met Jesus. He reached out for her and lifted her up from the abyss. Once again she could see the beauty of life around her. Hers was a simple faith. Like all those who have deeply suffered, she only knew that it was nourishing to be near her Savior. She followed him in his ministry, including the great journey to Jerusalem.

But her bright world had been shattered on that fateful Friday. Jesus had helped her find great strength in herself. She used it as she stood like a rock near the cross. She was there until the end. Then the old wounds in her soul began to tear apart again under the strain. However, she was used to darkness and she remembered the words, the looks, the prayers and the touch of her beloved Jesus when he had given her a new life. Slowly she climbed back into the light. Life must go on.

She was the first to go to the tomb and to be amazed at its emptiness. What does it mean? The great forces of the world had decided to rid themselves of the irritation of this one called the Christ. They killed him. Surely they had won. Had they not?

You would have to be insane to believe that somehow Jesus had not been destroyed. But Miriam of Magdala had been a bit insane and she was still crazy enough to believe, to have some absurd hope, that the gentle Kingdom of God would continue.

And it has.

A Quiet Moment

RESPONSORY
From Phillipians 2:6–11

R. God raised him on high, alleluia.

His state was divine,
yet he did not cling
to his equality with God
but emptied himself
to assume the condition of a slave.

R. God raised him on high, alleluia.

He became as we are
But he was humbler yet,
even to accepting death,
death on a cross.

R. God raised him on high, alleluia.

But God raised him high
and gave him the name
which is above all other names.

R. God raised him on high, alleluia.

PRAYER
From the Book of Blessings *of the Canadian Conference of Catholic Bishops*

All glory and praise are yours,
ruler of heaven and earth:
We praise you for raising
your Son Jesus from the dead
and for giving him victory over sin.
Make us holy as we follow him in love,
and fill us with your Spirit,
so that we may give you glory
all the days of our life.

R. *Amen.*

XIV *Jesus at Emmaus*

That very same day, two of them were on their way to a village called Emmaus, seven miles from Jerusalem, and they were talking together about all that had happened. Now as they talked this over, Jesus himself came up and walked by their side; but something prevented them from recognizing him. He said to them, "What matters are you discussing as you walk along?" They stopped short, their faces downcast.

Then one of them, called Cleopas, answered him, "You must be the only person staying in Jerusalem who does not know the things that have been happening there these last few days." "What things?" he asked. "All about Jesus of Nazareth," they answered, "who proved he was a great prophet by the things he said and did in the sight of God and of the whole people; and how our chief priests and our leaders handed him over to be sentenced to death, and had him crucified. Our own hope had been that he would be the one to set Israel free. And this is not all: two whole days have gone by since it all happened; and some women from our group have astounded us: they went to the tomb in the early morning, and when they did not find the body, they came back to tell us they had seen a vision of angels who declared he was alive. Some of our friends went to the tomb and found everything exactly as the women had reported, but of him they saw nothing."

Then he said to them, "You foolish men! So slow to believe the full message of the prophets! Was it not ordained that the Christ should suffer and so enter into his glory?" Then, starting with Moses and going through all the prophets, he explained to them the passages throughout the scriptures that were about himself.

When they drew near to the village to which they were going, he made as if to go on; but they pressed him to stay with them. "It is nearly evening," they said, "and the day is almost over." So he went in to stay with them. Now while he was with them at table, he took the bread and said the blessing; then he broke it and handed it to them. And their eyes were opened and they recognized him; but he had vanished from their sight.

Luke 24:13–31

A Quiet Moment

REFLECTION

Once again we are at the Lord's table. Now, as he did a few days before, he breaks the bread and we see him again. He is with us in all the ordinary moments of life as we walk and work. We usually do not see him because we are preoccupied with many trivial cares. Nonetheless, when we cry or laugh he is there. When we face the stone wall he is ready to lift us over.

As we gather around his table it is easier to become truly aware of our brother's presence. When we realize that he is willing to become a part of our whole existence we feel his peace washing over us once again. In that inner quiet we understand his desire for our age. He would like to act through us to bring more love and joy to the life we share with all our brothers and sisters in the world. He would like us to be yeast in the bread of life.

We are each invited to continue his glorious resurrection by spreading his light into the dark corners, his peace into the pockets of turmoil, and his gentle grace wherever it is needed.

A Quiet Moment

RESPONSORY
From the Didache

R. To you be glory for ever!

We give you thanks, Our Father
for the holy vine of David your servant
which you have made known to us
through Jesus.

R. To you be glory for ever!

We give you thanks, Our Father
for the life and knowledge
which you have made known to us
through Jesus.

R. To you be glory for ever!

As grains have been gathered from many hills
to form one bread
so may your people be gathered, Father,
into your Kingdom.

R. To you be glory for ever!

PRAYER

Our Father, who art in heaven, hallowed be thy name.
Thy Kingdom come, thy will be done on earth as it is in heaven.
Give us this day our daily bread, and forgive us our trespasses as we forgive those who trespass against us.
Lead us not into temptation, but deliver us from evil.

R. *Amen.*

**LET US GO FORTH IN PEACE AND IN LOVE—
THANKS BE TO GOD**

† † †